Too Much Water Will Kill The Flower

Calming the Chaos

Written by T. McGilberry

Unplugged Vintage Publishing ©2018

Cover Photography Courtesy of
Stanislav Kravchuk

ISBN: 978-I-949544-00-8

Never forget you're on a journey,
Even when you get there.

- T. McGilberry

Words for the Wise and Unwise…

For the lost and found...

To the spirit and
legacy of
Mark Early

Too Much Water Will Kill The Flower
is about self elevation.

You owe it to yourself.

Table of Contents

Bread Crumb

The coolest get cooler by the second,
The hot will make your heart melt.

The poetry is deeper when it's heartfelt..

The angry send a vibe to make the earth shake,
The depressed make you pity..

The sad will make you wonder why?

How do these different people bloom in the city?

Smalltowners with ambition no one believes in,
The humble great waiting for his door to open..
With no confidence to kick it in and play his token.

This game was made for all of us to play and win,
At some point..

Too many knowers and thinkers,
But no one begins.

Shadow Boxer

I'm like a wrecking ball to your concrete,
The wall shatters..
Crumbling any misconception before me.

Crumbling your hatred once you see my true spirit;
Your fear of what you could not comprehend.

The monster inside your brain,
Has kept you looking on the low-side of your bed,
and in the closet.

Your mirror cracked from disgust
and you refuse to fix it..

You can't hide from yourself,
Then blame it on everyone else..

The shadows of shame scream
"We don't believe you!"
You must have forgotten that a glass house is see
through.

Peeping through your peephole looking anxious..
Reading into rumors,
Living life in a bubble..

Pop it from the inside and step out!
Or would you rather wither away under the control that
has been placed upon you?

The constant programming..
Misguidement..
You mistake me as your enemy..

I'm not here to bring your life worry,
Talk back to the voices in your head to see what else
they can come up with.

I know you're angry,
Many felt that way before they grew.
Misjudgement can't get you far,
If you don't know who you are here's a start.

First Date

The ocean breathes a scent to make my mind peak,
The heavens shine and show me the way.

Today is one of many..

Yet it's one of one.

We may cry and laugh at the same time,
Some will watch others perform miracles.

The hard working and lazy all share the same 24 hours..

I've realized a thousand times my eyes may not tell me
the truth.

It's in my heart..

My heart will show me the way.

808

Drums beat..
They match my heart just not as loud.

I can feel the freedom,
The rhythm of liberation.

I sing to my soul's piano.

My inner stillness dances on the horizon.

Each step stretches my balance in a new direction.

Let the drums play..
Incarcerated spirits echo...

Let the drums play..

Follow your heart to the finish.

Oceans Eleven

Wanderlust,
Or lust for wonder..
I wonder.

Curiosity peaks,
But many of the answers I find..
were not the ones I seek.

Culture can come in different ways,
Constantly questioning how it should feel to be alive..

Do not let them sell you a dream from a slot machine,
Holding the handle to pick one after popping in a few
pennies..

There are things you have to work for,
Vacation is in the mind.

My curiosity arm wrestles with my consciousness,
My past is trustworthy to most,
But to those I hold close I still have much to prove.

Never to save face,
Sort of like a show and tell to let them know I care..
Not to show off or impress,
Simply to relay what we are made of..
To shine our true capabilities.

I've been mining in my mind for years,
Many gems have fallen off the back of my truck.

Many friends have grown from my light,
As I have from theirs..

And that is the way it should be.

Our minds are constantly impregnated..
Lay low with your flaccid facts.

You can double down back to back off my deck,
This hand I'm playing..

Is for the win.

Words from the Wishing Well

I don't know is not the final answer,
If you are searching for your destiny..

It is the question that sparks the journey.

Hold onto love,
Without it..
You are just another walking element,
Searching for which thou hath just lost.

The cycle will be slowed if you stop running.
Turn off that rat switch in your mind please!
That piece of cheese hanging from a string,
Is merely a reflection of what you already own.

We all want more..

There is honor in ambition,
I can collect achievements..
But nothing is more important than finding reason for
breathing.

There is still truth in humanity,
Yet we all struggle to find balance.

Searching for validation,
Searching for someone to love us like we love
ourselves..
To see what we see in the mirror.

I can't show you a picture of it but it's tangible;
Let the free flock together.

Let our hearts combine to make the Earth shine bright
enough to source light to another planet,
Giving the sun it's well earned rest.

I keep seeing these visions,
I hear of others having them too.
Too many of us lust for love and money,
But the truth can set our paths straight.

What do I really need to do today?

Snapping out of this trance of sedation..

When I feel danger I reflect,
Knowing I'm not finished..
And have no time to pretend.

I close my eyes,
To find that source,
To find that true alignment..

Of what really matters.

The Eagle Ascends

As I fly through these tunnels,
I see nothing..
But I feel everything.

The underground is cold and dark,
Yet it has a certain warmth to it..
A certain ease of comfort.

I keep my eyes low,
I know where I'm going..

Everything else is a distraction,
Disguised as something that I need or I should want.

I evade them all..

I don't need them where I'm going.

Maybe when I'm done,
I'll come back to dabble or indulge..
Grab a souvenir or two.

But right now it's strictly business,
Steadily making decisions..

The key to my freedom.

Not the American dream,
Far more simplistic..

Goals to grow thorough while staying centered.

I'm so close to the Earth I can almost feel it spin,
You may miss me from your arrogant view..

The Eagle Ascends...

Neo

Eyes open always..
But not too wide.

Too many distractions.
The road was paved to be traveled,
This life was made for you and me.

The life you live…
I'll let you ponder and complete the sentence.

Whether searching for secrets,
Or enjoying blatant truths hidden in plain sight..
This unedited movie script never stops.

One day I looked into the mirror
and seen a groundhog living in the matrix,
These days I sweat from liberation..
The odor isn't carefree it's carefully concocted.

Do you ever get tired of keeping track of irrelevance?

Think of everything you know,
And ask yourself if it amounts to anything?

One day you'll give birth to a blank slate,
And they'll need to know everything you really know.

How long will you distract them,
The same way you distract yourself?

If I were you I'd get a head start.
Begin by realizing what's really in your head,
and then start to live a real life.

Live a life worth laughing..
Why so serious?

Live a life where you have 5 minutes to help somebody
out..
And once you figure out what's really going on inside
your head,
Live life outside of it..

Because there's way more to be excited about.

You were only taking out the trash..
Trash you would have handed down to the next
generation,
As it may have been handed to you.

Damn it feels good to be a human being..
Reborn without re-entering the womb.

The matrix is a lot like high school..

You can tell who never left.

X

A poet society,
I write life not anxiety..

These permanent words,
On impermanent feelings..

Like seeds,
Begin hard..
Needing proper soil and water,
Solar energy for the bloom.

I write these words so you may know,
We too feel the same..
Even if unspoken.

And if we disagree,
Find another poet to light your Christmas tree..
Or at least heed my perspective as I did yours.

My mind travels full circle,
Only to express what is in the center of me..
Or slightly off.

Wherever you can find heart.

All hearts are not created equal.
Forgive me..

All hearts are created equal,
Yet some will grow while others shrivel..
Similar to the mind.

What separates us from the trees is we can always choose our
source,

Always..

Anyone who tells you differently,
Walk away swiftly..

Hopefully one day they may free themselves,
From their own self imposed prison.

Too many sit behind closed doors,
Not knowing they need no key for the lock..
Half the time we don't even need a clock.

Waiting for that certain moment…

If you're waiting,
You may keep waiting..

There is a difference from being persistently patient..

If you're moving forward I adore you..
Leave a mark so I know we've shared the same path.

These writings are my X for the next,

Traveling through these caves of life..

As we defer death's draft.

Remote Control

I daydream all day.

Some would call it living the dream,
But I call it daydream..
Because I do what I dreamed to do,
All day.

I didn't say I could fly,
And I don't think I'm better than you..
But I don't want to hear your stories of getting by.

I want to hear what you tried..

And if you did not almost die,
I want to know why you're not doing what you wanted to
do.

I did not drop out of my mother's placenta with an
agenda!
It took me years to face fears I didn't even know I
had..

But we have been programmed to be complacent..
It's time to grab the remote control,
and place it at your own skull!

What channel are you on?
Is it..

I know what I want,
I know what I need,
And **no** one can stop me?

Or channel…

That's ok,
Maybe tomorrow..

I think you're on channel I'm not good enough.

Or, I wasn't born with this..

I wasn't made for this.

Those channels always have the highest ratings.

Everyday your life is fading,
and not like the good looking haircut..

Save your woe is me and life sucks.

Oh, I know!

Your favorite channel is blame it on bad luck!?

Too lazy to change the batteries if you need to replace
them.

Look.

We all have choices,
We all have decisions to make.

I need you to stop surfing to the wrong channel.

Or better yet..

Just turn off the TV.

Monotony

Sometimes order is the death of stimulation..

Simulating through the basics..
My socks are sweaty, shirt dirty,
And my hands worn..

My brain is on fire,
Literally steam seeping through my pores.

Glorious times,
Not really knowing what I was doing..
But I was doing.

Some odd sort of preparation,
But I was ready.

While everyone was begging for reparations,
I was taking..
Picking fruit from high trees and bushes.

You sit down praying for things to get better,
My meditation is in motion.

Everyday I speak to myself..
To keep my eyes open.

Aware of what I see,
But not drawn into the magnet.
Your law of attraction is stagnant.

My passion for purism normally keeps me steady.

In between the cool air..
And the hot and heavy..

Comfort Zone

Slaughtered.
Beat to a pulp.
Skinned, tarred, and burned at the stake,
To an unrecognizable state.

Completely destroyed,
Not even left to be fed on.
I murdered mediocrity yesterday..

Have you heard the news?
What will you ever do without it?
It's no longer coming to look for you,
It's no longer in your corner keeping you comfortable.

It is gone..
The option is no longer available.
And if I ever see it again I'll do exactly the same
thing.

Death to mediocrity,
I slaughtered it,
Then I shot it twice in the head.

No funeral..
No ambulance came.
Everyone celebrated.

Hands in the air!

Let the trumpets sound.
Mediocrity is dead,
Find something else to live for.

Upgrade your guidelines.
Find something else to hide behind.
No new excuses.

Drop whatever you're doing.
If it isn't building greatness,
If it is holding you back,
Let it go.

I murdered mediocrity yesterday..
There were no flowers or balloons,
Just feelings of freedom.

What are you waiting for?
Stand empowered over your mediocre mind, mediocre body.
Grab the tools to your left and right,
And abandon your mediocre life!

My mind builds palaces wherever I walk,
Everything doesn't have to glitter with gold,
But everywhere must be filled with souls who still
believe there is more to the world than what you see at
the present moment.

Experience your imagination fully.

I murdered mediocre,
No thanks needed.
It was my pleasure..

Hands covered in blood,
I left the stains just so you can ask me what I've
done.

Mediocre was a coward,
A false facade,
Leaving you comfortable as you fade into nothing
but regrets of your own hopes and dreams.

Today I take a step towards life.
Today I build for tonight,
And tonight turns into tomorrow.

I will not sit and wait,
Unless patience is needed.
Mediocrity is dead.

Please do not stay seated.

Cocktail

I feel trapped in this body;
Introversion perversion.

I open my mind free to let the birds in..
They fly away looking for more.

Sometimes I'm visited by the eagles,
Other days pigeons drop shit.
Owls hoot in pursuit,
But this phoenix fire keeps me hot..

Ablaze throughout the day,
Dying to be set free.

Death never,
That is my last wish.

My existence is captivated by my environment,
My environment controlled by its creators..
And they seem to have run out of ideas,
If they ever had any.

This imagination time travels
smoothly through a town near you.
Who has the best food?
Who offers the most pleasure?

So many will do anything for change,
Even destroy everything around them
including the ones who love them most.

I wish this on no one..

The struggle between pain and pleasure deceives me.
Not knowing who to trust,
Not knowing who or what to love..

This world is not a straight shot,
It's a shaken cocktail..
With a splash of poison.

Not enough to hurt you,
Just enough to know it's there.

Some will add more to their drink to see what they can
take,
Some just want to escape..

But I want to be here,

Wherever that is...

Wrinkled Faces

Attitude painted across wrinkled faces.
Playing life,
Trying to circle the bases..

The basics weren't given in school.
Searching for tools..
Some words worth reading,
Actions worth repeating.
Swinging at objects that don't belong on the field,

Can you feel?

It's a twisted metal fallout,
Between the bots and the boys..
Many minds left to rot and decay.
Sedated on prescription pills just to brighten their
day,
Like the sun came out and had nothing to say..

We are beautiful people;
Damned and misguided.
Trying to control our wings as we pilot..

Pride beaming out the side of our eyelids,
Projects posted..
Hey!
Look what I did!

We are building the future of the future,
The culture of the new age.
Young and powerful,
Old and active.
Thou shalt never lose thy spirit..

We are an accumulation of moments,
False identities chosen, some unchosen.
Skin color and religions confuse us..
When we don't unite,
Everyone loses.

Except those who planted the seed of separation to
begin with.

The hate breeders..
They plant a seed,
Then teach one to reach many.

Some of us are infected..
If conflict resolution were as profitable as war,
There would be peace.

We could be the missing link to put the pieces
together.
We could do that without being told..

There is no **power** without the people.

African America

Many hopes and dreams sleeping in blood puddles.
No mastermind to call the play;
No quarterback to save the day.

Walking around in trances,
Unwilling to take chances..
The wrong move could mean we don't eat the next day.

My culture was left to the vultures.
They grind us up for crust,
Bake our bodies then masquerade
"In God We Trust."

But trust this..

If you eat me,
I'll poison you from the inside.

I move like I have lion pride,
While my ego remains atom size..

The basis of all being,
It's everywhere..

Yet you don't see it.

You talk a mouthful but you won't want to eat this,
History will repeat this.

With every moment being history,
I repeat this.

I will **never** die.

I Will Never Die.

Kill my body I've already sparked the next mind.

They left my culture to the vultures.

Capitalistic but maybe not to their own falter,
They probably had something to prove to their own
fathers..

But now we lay as sacrificial lambs at the altar.

Where are we?
Why do we lie here to be eaten?

The whips have been ripped apart,
Yet I still feel beaten..

You don't know what you don't know,
But if you don't know your history,
They'll repeat it.

Like it's a new secret with a new twist.

So I'm not sure what to recommend you,
But **this just in..**

We're all still on the menu.

So either we learn to cook,
Or be another burned history book.

They left our culture to the vultures..

I hope I'm not the only **eagle.**

Anonymous

Substance lacks abuse.
We find purpose on accident.
History repeats itself.
But we never know where time loops.

Substance.
Lacks.
Abuse.

We find purpose on accident.

History repeats itself..

But we never know where time loops..

Dawn

I have plans that need to be followed,
Pride that needs to be swallowed..
My ego is an eagle,
Going on a downward spiral.

Hunting that worm in a book,
That golden nugget of knowledge.
In my heart,
I believe every man shall prosper..

But only if he really wants it.

My eyes tell me differently.
I see struggle teeter up and down like a see-saw,
I meet dumb rich,
and smart poor on a daily basis..

Which interferes with my filter on how to really make
it.

Luckily I've already begun to clear my own path.
I know making it doesn't exactly mean riches..

To me it's the chance to create opportunity,
And connect with others visions.

To me it's not asking for permission.
Every man wasn't made to run a business..

But every child is born with ambition
to carry out their crazy wishes,
And somehow I never lost that.

Though sometimes I can't even tell you what the wish
is.

They aren't words,
These are feelings when my mind is open..

You understand the vibe,
Though it's unspoken.

Something universal as the sunrise.

There's something in the air today..
I can feel it and I can see it.

The mirror won't show you,
Even those that know you..

Just **be** it.

Sponge Water

Out of my head,
I pour out what I've absorbed..
Much good, much bad,
Now I'm here to make sense of it all.

A lot of life is grey from the black versus white,
To say who's right or wrong
May come at the end of the song..

But times change and the music certainly does too.

Don't even ask my opinion on the radio.
TV was cool until the Internet..

Now you can't hide the truth.

Most people don't want it but I do,
Straight like whiskey or tequila shots.

We are obese from the sugar coat,
Individuals eating lies like candy..
Just so we can feel good.

You and I both know,
But who's going to say it first?

Whoever has the least to lose.

Blue Paper Blues

Consumed by responsibility..
I couldn't wait to grow up.

Sometimes I hold my hand to my ear..
Searching for the world say "Thank You."

Thank you for coming,
Thank you for showing up..
Thank you for keeping me running.

You see what's the world without people?
No one that I know asked to be here..
We don't even know how,
Or where we've come from.

Different theories tested,
Proven maybe..
But who really knows?

Sometimes I feel the Sun should say my name.
I mean it shines on me all of the time..
I know I am seen.
I know the Sun is aware of what happens under the
light..

I want to grab a moon's rock to etch in all of our
names,
As we follow it into the night.

I couldn't wait to grow up,
And be one of the stars free flowing through the milky
way..

But responsibility is consuming me,
Constantly clipping my wings..

The day is over,
I feel accomplished because I've completed all my
responsibilities..

But I really haven't done.. **Anything.**

I'm still living for the dollar,
That painted piece of paper..
The tastemaker,
Pacemaker of our society.

If you are making it then you should sit back quietly..
If you are not then we should rise up and riot?
Please!?

Are these really the only dreams we chase?

What do all the kids say?
I want to be rich with a big house..

What if they were born with that?

Does that mean they have nothing to live for?

I'm still chasing the dollar..
Guilty.

Honestly I'll probably die filthy..
But was this really the only dream?

I couldn't wait to grow up.

School is Out.

Our thoughts burn,
We let the flames engage us.

I don't have time to prove myself to you strangers..

I'm just another member of the team pushing the
culture,
We caught a flat awhile back..
A few more dollars for the starter.

I refuse to get slaughtered.
My manners were so polite after I slapped you.
This isn't something you grab and nap to,
This is what you read when you're tired of being a
statue.

Some of the laws and statutes you abide by,
We may not share the same vision.
I would be lying if I said I only did it for the
children.

I wanted it yesterday,
Then I made my decision.
Some lazy leader told me to wait..
I looked away before I turned to slate.

Another rock thrown in the ocean,
Making a ripple with no true effect.

They want a world of just themselves until there's no
one left.

Copy me! Copy me!
Copy me!
Be the one to so there's no more three.

Three was company,
Accompanied by love, peace, and unity.
They prefer us in each other's faces.

Separatism.

The difference between me and you,
So many differences between me and you..

True human souls born,
Clones set as their replacements.
This social programming degrades us.

School is out.

Perfecto. (Generally Speaking)

Thinking,
I know what I was set here to do.

But that would be a lie.
I could think of vast things like
"be great,"

But then I would ask why?

Looking for something specific in a general place,
Generally everything is the same.

Same general places,
People with general names,
Same general channels,
To gain general fame,
Which still brings the same general feeling..

The one we all share,
The one that whispers in our ear
There's just a little bit more.

All searching for the secret that lies within,
Willing to turn ourselves inside out,
Generally speaking of course..

Just to find it.
Perfection.

Or something to make you feel that way,
Or something to make you look it.

Imperfection is perfection.
That's the only thought that stops the cycle,
The dog from chasing its tail.

We may never be complete,
Because life isn't..

Except complete utter chaos.

But generally speaking..
That's what makes it and **us** perfect.

Minutemen

Enlightening as the time bends..

The clock watches,
But you stare back as if it were a contest.

Time is man made.
A state of mind for the organized,
Kryptonite for the lost..
Possibly non-existent for the free.

Your invisible chain goes tick tock.
Put your hands around the clock,
Set it yourself.

You make the time..
It doesn't make you,
So show yourself a good one.

The Altar

A world full of open doors is an
unsecure place.
If you are too lazy to twist the
knob,
You do not deserve what is in
store for you.
If you are too afraid to twist
the knob,
Then maybe you should put a ring
on fear's finger.
Obviously that's who you would
love to spend the rest of your
life with.

Orphan Glory

So many kids are forgotten,
They are not victims..
They are symbols of strength.
Delicate candles that may be
blown out in moments,
but have unlimited wick,
Unlimited wit,
Unlimited grit..
Kids never quit,
Light them as they show us the
way.

Night & Day

This world I live in is unprotected,
Egos flying everywhere.

The soil is soft,
There's no foundation..

Some lie, cheat, and steal to stay alive,
While others lie, cheat, and steal to feel alive.
We play the game differently..

Givers win.
Takers only end up taking from themselves,
Sacrificing future opportunities for temporary gain.

Some say love is blind,
But in my world it keeps me sane..
The others never had much to show.

The beauty around me is overwhelming,
Physical and spiritual.
I'm now a product of the environment I placed myself
in.

The sun still shines in darkness.

Nameless

I met a dummy with a gun,
Said he would kill for fun.
Most of his actions we shunned,
He never had any fun so..

He loaded his magazines and begun from Day I.
Anyone who made him jealous,
The story he would tell it..

Such a lonely victim in his own right..
Mistaken misfit,
Outcasted by his own doing.

He wasn't even original.

The puppy that didn't get enough petting,
Now holds the power for tonight's setting.
There are a million things you can do in this world to
get noticed..
But he decided to plague us.

All these years of silently begging us,
But no one cared.
That's life though, right?

I can walk down the street and no one will notice me,
Won't stop me from getting something to eat.
But this dummy with a gun wanted to kill for fun..

Maybe for some fan mail,
Or his name in a book.

Question though?

Can you name anyone outside the 20th century known for
killing for no reason?

Your pitiful story will get lost in seasons,
You sick bastard..
Coward.
Go cry at the beach,
Maybe the ocean will soothe you..
A bikini body walking by to ease the pain.

I met a dummy with a gun,
Who would kill for fun..

All because no one knew his name.

Potent Paths

Today I saw some opportunities,
And I grabbed them.

Today someone tried to tell me what it was,
And I showed them what will be.
All that talk you do,
If I lit a match -- the room would blow.

Life isn't up for discussion,
It's up to the movers and the makers..
Everything in between will be squeezed.

Every pair of eyes wants to make it to that one point,
That place is different yet inside all of us.

Whether we make it or not,
Is the difference between potential..

And potency.

Be a bridge,
Not a stoplight.

Full Spectrum

I'm done with limits.
My existence alone is limited and I don't know why.

You should know me,
And I should know you the same.
Yet somehow I didn't get your name because I didn't
ask.

I didn't ask for this day,
It was given.
For that I am grateful because nothing else is.

Maybe more would be if I could take advantage of this
one thing..
This one thing called Time,
I'm beginning to manage.

It's a lot harder because it keeps showing up,
Even if you don't work for it.

Everyone wants you to spend it like they do theirs..

But my time is like a color that hasn't been discovered
and I'm still trying to find it a name.

Quick Draw versus Cecil Scope

Life is chasing life.
Abilities unknown.
We get to know life..

Some weaker, some strong.

Some will show life,
Some will show life life,
Then new is sprung.

Slow to fast,
Fast to slow.

Life is something makers know.
Consumers drive us crazy,
But we cater.

Bored minds,
Acting like they're owed life,
You have no right.
It can take less than two hands to make your own life..

To those who live a so-so life,
I'm so-so tired of comparison..

Winners are losers too,
We don't quit.
Trying to catch a break?

Maybe you should pick up the ball and decide who throws
and who catches.

You could be a master.
Maybe..

At first you could be a disaster.

Maybe..

Life could go right,
Life could go wrong.

Nothing really stays or leaves,
Everything rearranges.
Even proximity changes..

Rome is everywhere.

Life is lived and perceived.
Life is lived, dreamed, and redeemed.

I had two tickets to the gun show,
Ended early because Quick Draw was sniped by Cecil
Scope.

Life is life,
If you must fight..
Get off the ropes.

Unless that is a part of your strategy.

Inside Jokes

The art of life,
Sometimes holds concealment..
Everybody doesn't have to know.

Most that advertise,
Don't do half of what those do in silence..
Yet they receive all the praise.

Everyone wants to be like the one
You don't really want to be like…

Makes me laugh every time.

Reset (Status Quo)

If I were to tell you I was...
You wouldn't believe it.

Because we have gotten used to our friends not
achieving,
Everyone just getting by..
Feeling underwater,
And barely breathing.

I say we change the status quo,
And break even.

Waiting for another day to become your day..
You watch television,
Go to sleep..
And dream your dream life all over again.

It's to the point where you won't even tell a friend
because it's unbelievable.
But let me tell you a secret..

There's a lot of money,
There's a lot of opportunity..
And we are being **lied** to.

Life is on the map for those who want to find it,
I never said the trip was easy.
I said anywhere you want to go is believable,
And there's probably someone who's been there.

Stop asking everybody who's never done it how to do it!

You can fail,
But within time,
You can only fail so much..
Before you get it right.

Every failure should teach you something the average
amateur wouldn't know.
You won't get your edge until you step off the ledge..
I hope your wings are ready.

When you take off,
And the clouds are in your face.
And you begin to feel the warmth of a closer sun..
You're going to remember what it felt like to walk.

.

You're going to remember what it felt like just to talk
about it.
Laughing at the fear that held you down,
As you now float on next to nothing but your own
strength.

If you told me you were…
I'd ask you how you did it.

Let's change the status quo together.

Your dreams have been driven off-road,
But they make tires for that.
They even make sealants and plugs for the flat.
Helicopters with ropes for those fallen in pits..
Even audio books for those who can't read shit!

For anything that falls apart,
There is a mechanic..
The biggest trees start from a seed,
Plant it.

You think your little mistakes will cause damage,
But everything you don't do is what ruins the planet.
Why else would you be here if not to change the world?
At the very least add to it.

Ask me for the right favor,
I'd be glad to do it.

Time… time… time…
All we have in this world.

Not waiting until the next moment,
My time is right now.
What do I have right now?
What can I do right now,
That will lift life for tomorrow?

Too many people die with nothing.
If I told you that you could be a living legend,

You probably wouldn't believe me..
It's time to change the status quo.

"The Perfects"

The perfects make the most mistakes.
Tried once,
Didn't get it right.
Tried twice,
Didn't get it right.
Tried three times,
Didn't get it right.
Tried four times,
Didn't get it right.
Tried five times,
Didn't get it right.
Tried six times,
Didn't get it right.
Tried seven times,
Didn't get it right.
Tried eight times,
Didn't get it right.
Tried nine times,
Didn't get it right.
Tried ten times,
Didn't get it right.
Tried eleven times,
Didn't get it right.
Tried twelve times,
Didn't get it right.
On the thirteenth try,
Was it perfect?
No.

But to the person who tried once it almost looked that way.

For Granite

You should be a skyscraper,
Foundation firm..
Wind never swaying you.

You as an airplane can maintain turbulence,
No black box needed.
Foggy nights bring wet mornings,
But you won't slip..
You know what's due.

You should be a skyscraper,
Built up at the highest heights..
But your architect doesn't have a clue.
The workers are inconsistent,
The plan is beautiful..
But they never follow through.

You should be a skyscraper,
But you lay as a brick in the bushes..
Waiting to be threw.

Cracking glass,
Joining riots..
Looters and shooters.
Causing all of these broken pieces on the ground.

The city wanted you to be great,
Now you're another piece of slate..
Hoping to be made in the next town.

Off Day

Off center,
Off base..
Shots missed.
Some people don't want to feel good.
They say life is evil.

They take advantage of your kindness and weakness,
Greed and your ego.
They take advantage of your street smarts,
And your book knowledge.
Lust will find you shot, stabbed,
Or worse..
Pierced from the soul.
Or maybe we're just losing control?

We've been sold these financed dreams,
They sell us dreams that aren't our own..
These dreams we can't afford,
Distracting us from life's true benefits.
We walk sleep,
And when we close our eyes what do we really see?

Darkness is upon us,
They tell me life is evil..
But wanting to skip levels is when you really meet the
devils.
They take advantage of your ambition,
Your wants and needs..

Take advantage of you when you're deep in shit,
Piss on you when you're in need.
You took a shot and missed,
And now you're off beat..

Afraid people are watching and listening.
Give them a show if you want,
But really know what you want..

Don't lose yourself if you don't get it today.

Only

Souls match.
Some vibes are hard to swallow,
Inhale my energy as you breathe..
Feel my being.

Attitudes distraught,
Shots through the night..
To the heart and the mind,
Concealing light from the blind..
Misjudgement matters of all mankind.

Two shots to the heart,
To an even worse extent we kill ourselves.
Souls bleed,
Discontent progression..

Who really holds the weapon?
Who really holds the power?
In whose hands will we believe?
Everything is in **us**,
The power to create..
The power to divide,
Bodies made of ice..
Only eyes seem to be alive.

Senses dulled or over stimulated,
Panic or peace?
Individual or whole?
Somehow we forgot that we sprang from the same mold.

Same story told,
Different names, ages..

Worth defined by wages.
Money is power,
Power is what we perceive.

We are the only ones who pay to be here.

We are the only ones who pay to be here..

We are the **only...**

Distressed

I never claimed to be the perfect person,
I never did all the right things either..

Don't judge my journey like you do yours,
We're cut from a different cloth
To make the same shirt.

Life is going to wear us out anyway..

Might as well make it funky.

Lost Souls II (Pyramids)

Lost souls,
Wrapped in gold..
Pyramids turned upside down.

I've come a long way from a few days ago,
Tongue uplifted a few prayers ago..
My soul seeks redemption peeking through these narrow
eyes.

There is a world in front of us that we do not see,
The secret is in the safe..
And even those who know,
Are not.

Lost souls,
Wrapped in gold..
Pyramids turned upside down.
Repetitive cycles..

Was the world greater at one point than it is today?

Was everything lost?
Are we some sort of experiment?
Dumbed down nations,
We grow to achieve things that have already been done,
Why?

Is the truth so bright it will blind us all?

Lost souls,
Wrapped in gold..
Pyramids turned upside down.
Living in this untold fairy tale,
If I cracked the globe would I be free?

Not waiting to be shaken,
Never knowing where the story ends..

Tunnel Visions

Maybe I should just paint the walls in this tunnel,
Create my very own Sistine.
Who says I need to leave?

Maybe this tunnel is my home.

Who cares what lies on the outside world,
If everything comes through me?

Weaving back and forth,
I'd rather stay centered.

Learn your game or create my own,
I'm a winner either way.
But there's magic in this tunnel,
Experiences some have felt in other parts..
And some none could ever imagine.

I could take as long as I want,
That's the beauty held in the hands of the creator.

Molding a life that could never be hardened like clay,
A modern day alchemist.

Who will turn their little life of coal
And make it gold?
Who will walk the path of the undistracted to create
what everyone has yet still seeks..

Life.
We can never get enough of it.

Heretic.

Lost in the lust of life and shiny objects,
A walking, metal detecting, gold star seeking,
Dull as a butter knife rubbing you up and down to get a
slice of your bread,
Making you dinner,
Just to poison you by dessert sweet talker..

My wish is to never meet this man in the mirror.

One day he shall lie lost and found in a plain box with
two words engraved;
Soul less.

My wish is to never meet a man that has never met
himself,
Plotting on everyone else..
Never realizing they were only extensions of how he
would be living if he walked their path.

I love life in a way a child loves his mother even
after she abandons him,
The child learns to be strong..
Learning to see her in light of who she really is,
Not who he wants her to be.

I love life the way a boy loves his stern father,
But no longer seeks his approval.

Too many under attack not to have empathy,
Too many attacks..
Not to learn defense.

Many are on the fence about too many things..

Play the field and become your own star,
With no cheers or trophies.

Be blinded by your own light in the mirror..

Every morning is a genesis,
Every night a revelation,
But no one is coming to save you as you sleep.

Many will become who they thought they would never be,
That could be grand..
That could be dreadful..

The fate falls on you.

Brita

We are water,
Searching to be defined..

Looking for a boundary or structure to contain us.
Fluidly moving through the Earth in a formation we will never understand,
Poisoned by fear..

Filtered through faith.

Why Did The Chicken?

Cracks in the pavement,
From the roots in the trees.
The wisdom is growing,
There's a shift in the lifestyle..
More love,
Leading to a different kind of competition.
Not one of accumulation,
But how can I help my brother grow?

Not one to outshine,
But how can I shine my light on those trapped in lonely
attics and dark basements?
Even the blind in broad daylight?
The mindset isn't to build and destroy,
But to build and replenish an army of enlightened
soldiers..
No more sheep's wool for the enemy.

The enemy is ignorance,
Ignorance is the root of all evil..
The basis of all control.

They can't divide us anymore,
Only spreading out the strong..
Placing us where we needed to be,
But didn't have the means to do so.

The cards are in our favor now,
If you can't feel it..

You may be on the wrong side of the road.

To Be Continued

Every poem is a love letter,
Every step is my new favorite dance move..

Every choice is my favorite though it might be my last,
I'm not afraid to change it.

Every night I wash my smile so I can wear it again,
The next day it may be a little wrinkled..

Still no iron needed.

Laces tied,
The music is playing..

In a stride to be the best imperfection
God has ever made,
The ultimate art piece..

The one he wants to tell his friends about.

One of the greatest contributions
To humanity is the highway,
And they are always under construction..

Allow me to reintroduce myself as,

To Be Continued...

Eviction

Complex trial and error,
Addicted to the addiction..
I looked inside to see a whole new world evolved.

The chains are broken,
Yet at times my mind struggles to be free..
The irony of the only thing that can't be taken.

I commit one of the deadly sins each day,
Yet I remain alive..

God has his eye on me,
The devil attempts to caress.
They both live in my head,
But one doesn't pay rent..

I guess we all know who's about to get evicted.

Springing Through Life

An innocent pure blessing is birthed
into an Earth of sin,
Out with the old and in with the new.

Similar to the cycle of steaming hot summers,
Falling into a wicked cold winter..
Only for the seeds of spring to begin.

They grow and sprout resembling the infant marching
through the canal of birth,
Breaking through April's showers and blooming into what
may be..
The most precious sight ever seen.

What is new must be appreciated..
But respect is due to those who paved the way,
Then decayed only to be known as just a name to those
who **live** today.

After winter's moons come the soothing
sun of the spring.
Its rays go out with the days
And its nights take flight until the cycle restarts.

The infant's days become restless as its life springs
through the seasons..

Realizing its name is written on the guest list of
life's death list,
And will be buried under the snow
in life's cold cold winter.

Without delay the seed breaks through the shell,
With the aura of heaven's angel living in hell..

Walking unscathed through the summer flames,
falling days, and winter pains,
To fully season..

Even on a rainy day.

I know nothing...

About the Author

You can find **Tim McGilberry** driving his Impala around
Florida,
thinking of new content and probably eating.
Surfacing on the internet from time to time..

Like **T. McGilberry** on Facebook
Follow me on Instagram
And also Twitter as **@timcgilberry**

If this book touches you in anyway please let me know.
Feel free to talk about some of your favorite pieces,
share some excerpts and tag me in them!
More work on the way..

For a **free bookmark and sticker** subscribe
for email updates on **timcgilberry.com**

Any feedback can be sent to **timcgilberry@gmail.com**

If you enjoyed this book please leave a review on
Amazon or any platform of choice..

Or don't tell anyone and we can form our own secret
alliance…

Oh and umm.. write your own poetry and draw on the
blank pages. Lets collab. Send me our collaborations.

Prints, shirts, other goodies coming soon
check the website & Instagram for details

www.ingramcontent.com/pod-product-compliance
Lightning Source LLC
Chambersburg PA
CBHW020551030426
42337CB00013B/1053